Fatherless Son:
Seven Penitentiary Numbers,
Captured by the Holy Ghost

Author: Charles Peter Winston
Writer: Nichole Sherrie Hickman
Illustrator: Steve Rountree

To the love of my life, Shurnie, and our
beautiful daughter, Shonnon

Table of Contents

Introduction

In my years of ministry experience in the area deliverance, I have seen the Holy Ghost do great things in the lives of many. Indeed, Chuck is a true testimony of the awesome power of the Holy Ghost to cleanse and deliver from the demonic oppression that kept him bound for years. I praise God for using me to help Chuck find the help he needed to free him to do the will of God in the earth. His testimony has truly led hundreds of captives to freedom and will, no doubt, lead countless others to enjoy the same victory in Jesus Christ over the power of Satan.

As you read this book, you will see the Spirit of God at work in Chuck's life. Although he was oppressed for years by demonic spirits, the Holy Ghost captured him and freed him as he surrendered.

If you find yourself in a similar situation, gripped by the power of darkness and struggling helplessly to get free, know that the same Holy Ghost power that led him to freedom, spiritually and physically, is no respector of persons. Surrender all to Him and let Him change your life as He changed Chuck's.

Deacon Ted Aikins
Local Church
Dayton, OH

CHAPTER 1
FATHERLESS SON

As a young child, life was sweet. I cherished time with my parents and they seemed to enjoy one another. We lived a happy family life together until the age of six when my father began to shift his interest from our family to the streets. His dealings in the streets left him extremely angry. Often times, his anger got the best of him and manifested itself in outbursts of violence directed at my mother and me. My mother and I escaped to her parents' house in fear to hide out in order to dodge his fits of rage. He figured we were there and followed and bullied her parents to the point where they became fearful of him, too. After several incidents of domestic violence involving the police, my mother decided to leave the home and the marriage. She obtained a restraining order against my father and eventually divorced him. In spite of my father's verbal and physical abuse of my mother and me, I hoped that he and my mother would reunite. However, to my dismay, sometime after the divorce my mother elected to move on with her life and remarry. For the next few years, I felt displaced, lost. I felt like a fatherless son.

At the age of eleven, my life began to take a downward spiral. I began to try to fill the void prompted by my parent's divorce in ways that caused me lots of trouble. One day, I was caught drinking and smoking on school grounds. My mother was called to the principal's office where she was informed of my behavior and consequences. She was very disappointed at my behavior and at the principal's decision to suspend me. However, I was even more devastated over my consequences than was she and became very depressed and suicidal. I contemplated suicide and expressed my desire to die with words like, "I want to be dead," and "I'm going to kill myself." My mother, having never experienced this type of behavior from her child, feared for my life. School authorities

Peter at age 11.

were concerned as well and demanded that I have a psychological evaluation before returning to school. In desperate need of help, my mother made an appointment for me to see a psychiatrist for an evaluation. After conducting several tests, the psychiatrist determined that I was simply acting out for attention. And over the next several months, I began to act out more and more. I returned to school and continued to drink and smoke on school grounds. I cursed out the teachers and bullied other kids and neighbors in the community. By the age of twelve, my behavior landed me in the juvenile detention center time and time again. My mother left me in the detention center on one occasion until she could determine what to do with me. She could find no way to make me obey her nor the law!

In the juvenile detention center I befriended boys who had similar behavior problems. Many were gang members. We became partners upon our release from the detention center and began to engage in criminal behavior as a group. We stole cars, snatched purses, held up department stores and skating rinks. We rushed into the neighborhood streets and terrorized motorists, picking up their cars while they attempted to drive way! We were totally out of control.

Needless to say, my behavior never filled the void in my heart of fatherlessness. This void drove me to commit bigger crimes the older I became. Very quickly I became discontented with the high from stealing cars and snatching purses so I began to commit robbery and theft in local businesses to support myself. The streets became my provider, not my parents. School was such a bore that I skipped class. Drinking and smoking cigarettes lost its ability to thrill me so I began to smoke marijuana instead. Not long after I picked up the habit of smoking marijuana, I discovered that it was a costly habit to maintain so I began to think of how I could earn the money to support my pot binges. I realized that marijuana was a hot commodity on the streets and that if I sold it I could earn the money to buy more to smoke. I hooked up with older men and women on the streets who had access to the stuff. They put me on the streets selling not only marijuana but also pills and whatever else I could get my hands on.

By this time, my mother and stepfather were thoroughly displeased with me and still could find no way to discipline me. She and my stepfather were at their wits end. They sent me to live with my grand-parents hoping they could curb my behavior. This arrangement proved fruitless as well as they could do nothing to convince me that I should live up to their expectations for me. I was empty, hurting, and angry and made up my mind that I would live life on my own terms!

My life was a mess! I began to sneak out into the streets until the wee hours of the morning night after night with my delinquent friends. Of course, my parents gave me a curfew but I disregarded it altogether. I crept out of my window when they turned in for the night to meet the fellows for another night of roguish antics in the neighborhood streets. Our crimes continued to earn us scores of eventful nights in the juvenile detention center. To add even more depth to the ditch I was digging for myself, I became interested in the opposite sex. I was a young teen by now, about thirteen, and found myself engaging in sexual activities with various women. Most of the women were about ten years my senior but seemed to have no problem contributing to the delinquency of a minor!

CHAPTER 2
A SEED IS PLANTED

One day while in the juvenile detention center, I met a man named Phil. He was a godly man who took an interest in me and showed me the fatherly love I missed so dearly. He took me and other troubled boys on outings to the local Salvation Army to play basketball. This was big fun for me since I had been banned from extracurricular activities like basketball in school a few years back. The boys and I were so good at basketball that we ended up playing on a team. Our team won several games that carried us all the way to Michigan for a basketball tournament! I began to have the kind of fun all kids should experience at that age. The boys and I were so excited about the fun we were having but did not quite know how to express it appropriately. We showed out so bad a few times that Phil stopped the vehicle on the highway to pray to get us back under control!

We knew that Phil was a "holy roller" so we used his faith to get to go on outings with him on a weekly basis to get a break from the detention center. Phil also used his time with us as an occasion to share his faith through group Bible studies. He planned a camping trip once. On one particular occasion, I was out in the woods with one of Phil's volunteer team leaders named Glen. This man took an interest in me and showed me fatherly love and concern just as Phil did. While we were sitting and enjoying the great out-doors, Glen said, "Charlie, I believe the Lord wants to touch your life, young man. But there are some things, Charlie, that you've got to do and God said what you can't do He would do for you." His words caught my attention because I always questioned God asking Him, "Why am I here?" I always asked Him why my life was so troubled as a young boy, why my father was not around to show me love, to spend time with me, and to make me feel like a human being. So I began to listen.

He continued to talk and began to introduce me to a man called, Jesus Christ. I listened and lis-tened. He read Romans 10:9 and led me in praying the Sinner's Prayer. As I prayed at thirteen and a half years old something happened to me! My whole body went numb as I prayed and I felt as if the Lord Himself came down from heaven and said, "I'll be with you and deliver you and show you My salvation, Chuckie." I was so excited! I joined the other boys on the basket-ball team who were camping with us and told them about my experience. The boys laughed at me and told me that there was no such thing as salvation. The more they taunted me the more I began to believe them. As time progressed, I became discouraged and began to feel all alone in my decision to live for Christ.

The trip ended and Glen returned to his post in the military. I never saw him again. Before leaving though, he stressed to me again that there was a calling on my life and that if I would read the word of God, He would take care of all of my cares and burdens. I didn't quite understand how reading His word would take care of my cares and my burdens nor how to nourish this newfound Christian life. So I left it be and I began hanging out with my street partners and after a while, my enthusiasm for Christ faded. I became involved in criminal behavior yet again.

During this spree of criminal activity, my partners and I began to become more creative in our mischievous endeavors. The usual stuff was tedious. In order to amuse ourselves, we stopped in the neighborhood drugstores, stole cough syrup and drank it. We clowned and acted like fools! Our antics, though they were exciting at the time, still never filled my need for fatherly love and acceptance. After some time, I met a group of "cats" that belonged to the neighborhood gang. We rode around the neighborhood together after school until dark everyday looking for a good time. There was a community pool in the neighborhood that closed at dark. We wanted to swim one evening so we jumped over the fence that enclosed the pool to take a dip. We clowned around and clowned around until finally a fight broke out. I jumped in and while fighting, the gang members noticed that I could box pretty well. When the fight was over and things died down, one of the gang members said, "You'll play a great part in our gang," and the other members agreed. They encouraged me to go through the gang initiation. I did and passed and became a bona fide "Black Master." I hoped to find in this gang the love and acceptance I so desired from an older male figure. Not only did I find acceptance and love from the older guys in the group who were like a father and big brother to me, I also found numerous opportunities to take part in still more lawless activities. Together we engaged in gang wars. We would fight, chain, and shoot against other gangs. We obtained guns and tons of ammunition from the local pawnshops, gun shops, and homes we robbed, sometimes bursting through brick walls to get what we needed, leaving behind a path of utter destruction. With these guns and ammunition, we terrorized community businesses and organizations at gunpoint. We intimidated the citizens so badly that the we, along with rival gangs, were beginning to take over the entire city!

At thirteen (almost fourteen), I engaged in much more than the average thirteen year old in the 1970's. I left home, skipped school, lived in the streets, earned a criminal record, served time in jail, experimented with sex, joined a gang and the list goes on! However, in the midst of all of this turmoil, I also met and accepted Christ! The seed of the Gospel planted in my life by Brother Phil and Brother Glen in the midst of the hell I suffered (and caused) continued to germinate although it seemed to be smothered and snuffed by my sinful behavior. God protected His deposit in my life just as He promised He would although His handiwork was not evident at the time.

CHAPTER 3
DADDY'S BACK

Not only was He working to fulfill His promise to keep me in spite of me, He also answered my prayer to be reunited with my father! My mother felt that my father was most likely the only one on earth who could reach me especially since the lack of his presence in my life is what led my feet to choose the path of self-destruction soon after he and my mother divorced. She resolved to let me move in with him to help ease the perpetual migraine headache I caused her. In my estimation, this new living arrangement was perfect. I was overjoyed! I looked forward to the time my father and I would share alone, just he and I, catching up on the years we missed, throwing a football, wrestling, hanging out, talking. Oh how excited I was!

To my sheer surprise, things did not happen as I imagined. My father and I spent almost no time together. In fact, I saw him very little if at all during the week. I stayed in his home with his wife who bore the burden alone of caring for me. He came home for a few minutes here and there, sometimes near dawn, to take a bath, change clothes, or get money. On several occasions he dropped by on the weekends at three or four o'clock in the morning to get me and take me to hang out with him. He seemed to feel guilty for leaving me home all week with his wife. Each time I hopped in the car with him expecting to finally get to spend time with him but we always ended up at the local bar. Each weekend we hung out, he pulled up in front of the bar, parked the car, and rushed inside. I sat in the car for what seemed like hours before he came out again. In the meantime, he sent one of his women to the car every so often to give me a soda or to comfort me and keep me content while he partied the night away. At the time, I was so excited to get to see him that I didn't mind sitting in the car until daybreak as long as I had the chance to be in his presence, even if for a second or two.

After awhile, my father began to involve himself deeper and deeper into street life. He began to sell drugs and ended up going back and forth to jail. I moved back home with my mother and stepfather when it became clear that he was not capable of caring for me. I was very disheartened that things did not work out with me staying with my father but there was still hope that we could keep in contact. We did for a while but the contact was not very pleasant at all. It always centered around my behavior and, of course, at that time in my life I was not your typical "boy next door" so if and when my father heard from my mother concerning me it was not under good circumstances.

One day, my mother was totally fed up with my outlandish behavior in school. The principle called her and informed her that I was caught sniffing glue and smoking pot in the classroom. Yes, I became just that bold and unconcerned with my behavior or school authorities! It was also discovered that I had a .38 snub nose pistol in my locker! My mother resolved to call my father to handle this one. She told him of my behavior in school and that no one could do a thing to restrain me. He came to the school and took me home with him. When we arrived, he began to question me about my behavior. After a very short, unfruitful conversation, my father proceeded to pick me up and throw me to the ceiling. He didn't bother to catch me. He just let me hit the ground. After he finished throwing me around, he gave me money to catch the bus home. I was so shaken up that I was too afraid to stand outside and wait for the bus. I feared that he would come out after me and grab me again so I walked home although the distance was several miles.

This was not the only time that my father

grabbed me. Actually, he shook me physically quite frequently when I got in trouble with the law. When he realized this did not yield the results he anticipated, he began to promise me material things if I straightened up.

One year, I got into trouble again around the Christmas season. My father promised me a nice, big Christmas if I minded my manners. I managed to be on my best behavior for the first time in years and even surprised myself. I sat and waited for him Christmas day to come in the house with my gifts. I waited and waited only to find out that my father sold the gifts he bought me to support the drug habit he maintained behind closed doors. Although his intentions were good, I was devastated to say the least.

CHAPTER 4
ON MY OWN

By this time, I was extremely angry with my father and extremely fearful of him, too. Still, I hoped to at least keep in contact with him over the phone and to see him occasionally but this did not happen either. We lost contact altogether once again as the street life was more important to him than me. My father failed miserably to heal my heart. In fact, he deepened the wound he left when he walked out of my life. He was my last hope and my last hope failed me miserably! I made a vow to take matters into my own hands once and for all. I figured that in order to survive in life I would have to be a man and provide for myself. There was a huge factor that kept me from fulfilling this vow, however. I was only fifteen and at fifteen, I had no job and no home of my own. I remembered that the older women I crossed a few years earlier had means to take care of me. I used them earlier to experiment sexually and decided to use them once again to take care of me. With this clever idea in view, I proceeded to seek out older women.

There was a club in town where the younger crowd hung out. This club attracted the neighborhood thugs and the thugs attracted older women. These older women were intrigued with the dangerous lifestyle of the neighborhood bad boys so I knew I would have no problem getting their attention given my notorious reputation. I was picked up time and time again each weekend just as I planned by various women, some twenty-four, others twenty-five. These were more than mere "pick ups" to me. They were stable means of material support since my father wouldn't do for me. They invited me home to party and to satisfy them sexually in return for a place to stay, cash, food, and whatever else I wanted. I didn't want for anything.

I began to feel real cool, like a true "player." Life went on this way for a short period of time before I realized that I was not using these older women but that they were using me! I was not the player but the "playee!" I couldn't go on living this way so I turned to crime again to support myself. I was caught by the cops breaking and entering and my mother was called. This time she refused to come to my aid. She told the cops that I was in their hands and that she had finally had enough. I was turned over to the court system and given the choice by the court to go to the Boys Industrial School or Job Corps. I chose Job Corps, a government run program that helped youth earn a G. E. D., learn a trade, and get work. The Job Corps facility in Indiana had an opening and I was assigned a bed there.

My grandparents helped me financially to make the transition from the streets of Dayton, Ohio to the halls of Job Corps in Edinburgh, Indiana. This opportunity seemed promising. After I arrived three weeks later, my admissions counselor advised me of the trades in which Job Corps offered training. I elected to train to become an auto mechanic and began to study in this area. Things were going smoothly in my life for a change until I connected with a group of dorm mates from Chicago who reminded me of the life I left behind in Dayton.

These guys were up to no good. They were dope dealers. They also smoked the dope they sold. They offered me a job making quick money as an inside contact with potential dope customers at Job Corps. I accepted and quickly began to bring in the business they expected I would. I smuggled pounds and pounds of dope into the Job Corps facility in soap powder boxes. Of course, Job Corps employees never suspected dope to be smuggled in the facility in laundry detergent boxes. It was a cool way to disguise

the dope since the dope looked just like powder deter-
gent! I thought I was very clever and clever I was, as
I became the big time dope boy on the Atterbury Job
Corps campus!

During the height of my career as Campus
Dope Boy, my grandfather became ill. I felt I needed
to help take care of him to repay the debt I owed for
his and my grandmother's support of me through the
years. I figured the money I made selling dope would

help ease some of the financial
responsibilities they experienced so
I began to try to figure out how I
could care for him and continue to
supply the dope my customers in
Job Corps became accustomed to

Peter in his Job Corps dorm room.

buying each week. This was no
problem for me. I planned out my weekly schedule
perfectly. I went to my grandparents' home on the
weekend to care for my grandfather. While there, I
purchased marijuana and rolled joints to sell during
the week. When the weekend ended, I returned to the
Job Corps campus with the dope I prepared during the
weekend visits to my grandparents' home all prepped
to hit the market.

Business was good. I said business was good!

I made so much money that I no longer needed to study to graduate from Job Corps. I paid for the connections to have my exams graded and every exam scored a one hundred percent. Even the exam I took to measure my knowledge of mechanical skills in an auto mechanic shop scored a one hundred percent although I didn't have much time at all to study nor practice fixing cars because of my day job as a salesman. Nonetheless, I graduated. Well, let's say I was given a diploma because I certainly did not earn one to say the least!

After graduation, my career as a salesman boomed. I became so good at what I did that my work took me from the streets of Illinois to Texas, from Texas to New York, from New York to Michigan. At this time, I made the career decision to broaden my horizons to include a prostitution ring. I hired a group of women who traveled with me. They sold their bodies to men for money as we traveled from state to state, from truck stop to truck stop. They did whatever necessary to make money for me to buy more dope and to spend. And indeed, the money was cashing in!

Some of the customers paid by check. I forged some of the checks to increase my revenue. I became so good at forgery that I began to write checks to myself on my customers' bank accounts and forge their signatures! Yes, the money was cashing in! It was time to make yet another career decision to broaden my supply base. I began to sell not only marijuana, but also heroine, pills, cocaine, and guns, anything to make money. I even tried my hand at gambling to see if I could line my pockets with dough in yet another fashion. Money, money, money! It became my god.

I left Michigan and returned to Ohio to generate more customers in that state. I connected with dealers there to sell pills. I also made connections with my cousins who sold dope in Illinois to help maintain my customers there. I began to weave a bigger, thicker web for myself because of greed. Although I had enough money by this time to provide for myself as I vowed I would do after my father failed me, I wanted still more. I broke into businesses and cars and even became involved in armed robbery to heap more and more material goods for myself to no avail. I could not be satisfied no matter what I did. It never dawned on me that a father's love could not be bought, conned, nor stolen so I continued on this downward spiral until I ended up in jail once again. By this time, I was in my early twenties.

CHAPTER 5
PAYBACK IS MEAN

While serving time, my mother and two younger sisters visited me. During these visits, my mother talked with me about my behavior and plans for the future. She pleaded with me to turn my life around, to find honest work to support myself and to obey the law. Each time I promised her that I would straighten up. I told her exactly what she wanted to hear to ease her mind although I had no intention of living life as a law-abiding citizen. In fact, I was planning my next criminal move with the guys I met in prison once I was released. We were planning how we could become more finessed in the crime world in order to get more goods and to lessen our chances of getting caught. We also sharpened our fighting skills. The guys from Dayton fought against the guys from Cleveland until we established which gang ruled. These fights went on and on and were long and hard because no gang member was willing to give up life on the throne in "Thugdom" without a fight almost to the death.

After serving about a year and a half in prison, I was back on the streets again. Things didn't happen exactly as I planned because I met a woman, began to date her and fell in love. She had twelve or thirteen children (I lost count) fathered by several men and was ten years my senior but this didn't matter to me. I was in love with her and offered to take on the responsibility of caring for her and her brood. She became pregnant with my child, her thirteenth (or fourteenth), and I was truly hooked. She literally turned me out then stole my heart. I moved in with her and the

children and she quickly became a real companion, a woman after my own heart, and a true partner in crime. I would do anything for her and with her, including shoot drugs into my arms, something I had never done before. We robbed drug dealers together to support

Peter with mother & sisters during a prison visit.

our drug habit and eventually were on the run for crimes we committed together. We were a virtual Bonnie and Clyde!

During this time, I began to experience the meaner side of the consequences of crime. My father and I crossed paths again and began to get reacquainted.

Since our last contact, he had made a huge name for himself in the drug world. I had heard that he and a man had had a disagreement and had been feuding for some time. When the man and my father met one day, my father sliced him with a blade across the throat then down through his chest and left him for dead! Shortly after this near fatal encounter, my father planned a trip to New York to buy heroine to bring back to Dayton to sell. He stopped by my house I shared with my girl-friend and the kids with his brother to get some money on his way to New York. After getting the money and exchanging a few words, he and his brother left my house and were off to the Big Apple to close this major drug deal. Before hitting the highway, they decided to stop at the neighborhood gas station to fuel up. My father stepped out of his car and was pumping gas when suddenly he was shot in the back of the head, mafia style!

A week after we buried my father, in January of 1980, I was sitting in my living room next to my .357. Two brothers came into my house as if they were going to buy drugs. One of the brothers had a gun stolen from him by his cousin. His cousin told him that I stole the gun. His cousin was living in my house as I offered him a place to stay because he was homeless. Naturally, they believed I stole the gun because by this time I had a nasty reputation on the streets just like my father. The guys shot me as I was sitting on the couch. I got up to shoot back figuring that they planned to kill me but I fell under the stress of the gunshot wound. Assuming I was dead, the brothers ran out of the house. My girlfriend's oldest daughter saw me lying on the floor and ran into the street to find help. She flagged down the cops who came in to survey the scene and called an ambulance.

The paramedics arrived and pronounced me dead on the scene. I was rushed to the hospital and was somehow miraculously resurrected from the dead. The doctors who examined me informed me that I was permanently paralyzed and would never walk again. I also wore a colostomy bag and was told that it would also be a permanent part of my life. The doctors were amazed that I was not dead or at least a total vegetable due to the severity of the gunshot wound. Surely the finger of God was in my life protecting me. They explained that the bullet that almost claimed my life was lodged in my back and that there was a chance that I would walk again if I had it removed. I considered the pros and cons with my cousin who convinced me to go through with the surgery assuring me that I had nothing to lose and everything, seemingly, to gain.

I took his advice and scheduled the surgery. It was a grueling eighteen hours long. The doctors were surprised at my recovery since the disk in my back was completely blown away by the bullet. I attended my therapy sessions faithfully. Soon the colostomy bag was removed. Before I knew it, I walked out of the hospital on a cane. Yep, I walked out of the hospital, back onto the streets, and into the life of crime I left before the near fatal accident. And it was waiting for me as if I had never left.

CHAPTER 6
PRISON, MY FIRST HOME

I immediately picked up where I left off, was caught by the police, and incarcerated on what then was my sixth prison term. I hooked up with cats in jail while serving time and began to set up my drug operation behind bars. I sold heroine and cocaine and quickly generated more business than I imagined. Before long, it was evident that I needed access to a phone after hours so that I could make contact with the dealers on the outside. I managed to sneak into the attic of the institution with the help of several other inmates where we hooked up phone lines so that I had my own private phone in the institution in no time! The correctional officers were in on the operation. They purchased the drugs for me on the outside with the money I earned from drug sales on the inside. The inmates and the correctional officers were my faithful customers. I used the attic as an office suite and party spot as it was there that I sold the drugs then turned around and smoked and shot up the drugs I set aside for myself as a reward for my hard work. It's true; the correctional officers were as strung out on the drugs I sold as the prisoners and me, and I loved it! They became poorer and I became richer as sales were very good, so good that I was able to send money home to my family to help take care of them and to the cats on the outside with which I had connections in drug sales.

In the midst of all of this, somehow I was paroled and was back on the streets. Free, again, at last! And free in more ways than one. The relationship with the mother of my child went south while I was incarcerated. I was angry with her for refusing to bring my daughter to the prison to visit me and after awhile the anger turned to bitterness and my love for her waned. Eventually, the cops caught up with her and she was incarcerated. My daughter was placed with an agency after my attempts to gain custody of her due to my instability proved futile. Soon I lost contact with them both. Finding myself free of the responsibility of maintaining a relationship and fathering a kid, well 13 or 14 of them, I felt alone again. Desperately needing quick cash, I looked up my friend, Mari-Juana. She was waiting for me and promised to take good care of me. She delivered on that promise for the ends I made selling her earned me enough to recruit three women to work for me. With these three new employees, four including Mari-Juana, I operated a small prostitution ring, traveling from state to state, building clientele as we went. Life seemed to be going rather smoothly. I was back on track.

A friend of mine caught up with me between road trips and told me that he had a friend he wanted me to meet named Shurnie Cunningham. He described her as a nice young lady with stable employment. He also warned that she was "a little on the heavy side." I said, "Okay, I'll play her along with the other three women I have," thinking that she would be a potential lover and employee for my road show along with the other three. He arranged for a meeting and the instant I laid eyes on her I fell in love! We began to date and I quickly lost interest in the other three women I used to work the streets for me. Without a second thought, I shut down the prostitution ring, got rid of all three women, and secured a job as a dishwasher in a local hotel to win the affections of this girl who captured my heart.

I later learned that this Shurnie was a faithful churchgoer. She invited me to go to church with her and I accepted the invitation, pretending to be a Christian to win her heart. I did whatever she wanted me to do just to be in her presence. My efforts paid off as our relationship blossomed after a year of spending countless hours together and we decided to become husband and wife.

Upon announcing our engagement, Shurnie and my mother went out to choose a wedding dress. While shopping, my mother had a heart-to-heart talk with Shurnie. She told her about my past and that I was, essentially, no good, certainly not material for marriage. Shurnie was shocked to learn of my past and took heed. She broke our engagement and I was devastated. My cover was blown. All of the months I played "Mr. Christian" went down the drain in one shopping trip! I couldn't bear the thought of knowing that I lost the love of my life and could do nothing about it without help. So, immediately I turned back to what I knew to do best to pacify myself. That's right. I went back to using and selling drugs on the streets and from crime on the streets back into the slammer! This place was beginning to be my second, well first, home. I seemed to spend more time in prison than anywhere else!

I was released on parole and back on the corner of one of the busiest intersections in Dayton, Lakeview and Fleetfoot, when Shurnie and her friend recognized me. Shurnie called and I turned. We both stopped in our tracks, hurried toward one another, and embraced in the middle of the street. Immediately we decided to repair the damage my mother caused and to get married just as we planned. We vowed never to let anyone else interfere with our lives together. We planned our wedding and married in the summer of 1984. I found work and settled into an apartment with my new bride, intending to spend the rest of my life with her. Life couldn't have been better: I had a job and the girl of my dreams; but this marital bliss did not last for a good month and a half.

It was July 10, 1984. I was off of work that day and my wife took off of work that day, too, so that we could spend the day together as newlyweds. It was a beautiful day. I awoke that morning anticipating having a great day of freedom with my new bride. As I made my way to the bathroom to take a nice, refreshing bath, there was a strange knock on the door. It was the sheriff and the state highway patrol. Shurnie opened the door and asked, "Who are you looking for?" The sheriff answered, "Charles Winston. We've gotta have him." Shurnie told them I was in the bathroom and pointed them in that direction. They came into the bathroom and arrested me while I was in the tub! I was escorted to the patrol car and shoved in. Off we went to the Montgomery

County Jail with Shurnie trailing close behind. After reading me my rights, the authorities explained that a correctional officer was caught smuggling drugs into the prison and, upon questioning, disclosed that I was the kingpin of the whole operation. I was charged with seven counts of aggravated extortion against correctional officers and seven counts of aggravated extortion against inmates for the drug operation I organized and maintained while behind bars just before being paroled. I was also charged with one count of embezzlement. This charge was filed when it was discovered that another inmate and I called an elderly woman at random after hours while in prison and convinced her to send ransom money from her account in the form of money orders to his family and my family so that he would not be killed. She was so convinced that her money could spare his life and was such a compassionate lady that she sent large sums of money to the addresses we named. I was cruel! We arrived at the Montgomery County Jail where Shurnie learned of my charges. From there I was transported to the Pickwa County Jail. Shurnie followed. I was held there until my trial.

With all of the evidence leveled against me, I was convicted. However, the judge made a deal with me. He agreed to dismiss the seven counts of

Peter in London Correctional Institution (L.C.I.).

aggravated extortion against correctional officers and the seven counts of aggravated extortion against inmates if I paid back a portion of the money my jail mate and I conned from the elderly woman. I agreed to pay restitution. Shurnie wrote a check to cover the restitution costs from our family account and the charges were dropped. However, because I was on parole when the arrest occurred, the judge charged me with parole violation and ordered me to serve the rest of my prison sentence for which I was incarcerated before being paroled! So back I went to London Correctional Institution for 27 months, to life behind

Peter passing time on L.C.I. grounds.

thick, steel bars in a cold, dingy, rank prison cell. I was sick! I needed a change, a real change. The choices I made were now beginning to affect not only me but also my wife and I couldn't bear to see her hurt. I wanted for her to be happy, for us to be happy. I wanted to make a new home for myself, with Shurnie. I needed a true change, a heart change.

CHAPTER 7
HEART CHANGE GRANTED

L ife in prison quickly became routine. Outside of Shurnie's regular visits to comfort and support me, monotony ruled. One day, however, while walking down the corridors of the institution, I overheard a tape of a man preaching about Jesus and how this Jesus could help any situation, whatever the situation might be. The preach-ing gripped me. I asked the

Peter and Shurnie during a prison visit as newlyweds.

guy listening if I could listen, too. He invited me to sit, and as I listened, the word of God through this preacher man named R. W. Shambach penetrated my very being and pricked my heart to the core. The more I listened, the more I became convicted by the power of the Holy Ghost. I began to think to myself, "I can't read or write. I've been in and out of prison and can't seem to help myself. I need a change of heart. I've heard this Shambach preach about this man called Jesus. I will try this creature and see if He is able to help me."

God heard my thoughts and provided the opportunity for me to try His Son, Jesus. The Christian brothers in the institution came every morning at the break of day to the recreation area where the other inmates and I played poker to hold a Bible study. One morning I showed up and asked if I could join them. They welcomed me and gave me a Bible. Brother McGee, the inmate who led the Bible study, taught about Christianity and in no time, the brothers led me to Christ for the second time in my life.

I was ecstatic about my new relationship with Christ, my new Christian family, and my new Bible. I wanted to learn all I could about God. I looked at my Bible and prayed, "Lord, You've saved me. Now teach me, Lord, how to read that I might understand Your word." Once again, God answered my prayer. Brother Turner, another inmate, began to work with me and by the power of the Holy Ghost, Brother Turner taught me to read the word of God! The more I studied, the more I became a new creature in Christ. I felt as if I had actually been reborn. For the first time, I began to know God as a Father. I began to feel that I could call Him and depend on Him to be the Father I longed for over the years. I began to learn through the word that He was actually a Father to me all along and that through all of my troubles He was present although I did not realize it. I was so overjoyed. The word of God and His Spirit in my life changed me; I mean *really* changed me.

Over the next several months I continued to nourish my relationship with God. By the time the day of my freedom rolled around after my 27 months were served in full, I was so on fire for God that my wife hardly recognized me when she picked me up. I had changed so that she figured I had caught "jailhouse religion" or that I was "playing church." Time told a different story altogether!

I clung to my relationship with God once I was released for a good while and God kept me saved as He promised He would as long as I kept my focus on Him. I went to church with Shurnie and was introduced to her spiritual father, Ted Aikins. I knew how spiritually keen he was so I avoided him for five years. I knew he would see right through my shenanigans. Shurnie felt it was only appropriate for me to meet him. I agreed to do so, confident that I would pass his test since I was *really* saved now. He looked me over and shook his head. Later he called Shurnie at home to warn her about the struggles we would encounter over the next several years. To put it bluntly, he told her, "Sister, you've got yourself in a mess!" He also informed her that God told him that *he* would have to deal with me as well because I was going to be a permanent part of his life, too. "In one way or another," he declared to Shurnie, "God is going to use me in Chuck's life."

CHAPTER 8
CRACKED UP AND CRACKED OUT

Brother Aikins was right about the mess Shurnie had on her hands. Just as my family, friends and Brother Aikins predicted, I began to lose focus. I slacked up on my time with God, my testimony lost its fire, and soon I backslid. Like a dog returns to his vomit, I returned to a life of sin. This time I fell hard and deep. I began to drink gallons and gallons of alcohol. The liquor wasn't hard enough to drown my pain so I added crack to the fire and it burned me. I smoked so much "rock" that I became addicted and totally cracked out. I went to Florida with an uncle and there went buck wild drinking, smoking, and sexing! At times my body couldn't physically handle my binges and in an effort to calm my nerves, I rubbed all of the hair out of the back of my scalp. I finally cracked up! The demons from which I received deliverance returned sevenfold! I was worse off this time than I was at the first! And this time, Shurnie had had enough. She divorced me and I was left out in the cold.

I managed to secure several jobs while in Florida. I pressed clothes in a local dry cleaning store and was great at it but lost the job due to me party habits. I then secured a job picking apples. This job landed me in New York picking onions and unloading semi trucks in warehouses. Work was pretty good but my personal life was in shambles. Drugs where on every corner in New York and I bought as much as my money could buy. Soon the apple and onion season ended and I hit rock bottom. I was penniless and homeless. I ran into a couple of guys who lived on a farm in an old, run-down shack. I told them about my struggles and they invited me to crash with them until I could get back on my feet. I graciously took the offer to live on a farm, in New York, in a shack, with two guys, and no money to by a smoke or a hit. I couldn't believe my life had come to this. The big time kingpin was dethroned, a has-been, a bum.

Months passed and the apple and orange season peaked. Factories needed laborers badly so I found a job stuffing apples and oranges in fifty-pound bags and loading them on semi trucks. While walking down the highway to the factory to earn a day's wages, I was stopped by a gypsy named Ralph. He pulled onto the shoulder of the highway, rolled down his window, and hollered, "You look like you could use some work." I walked over to his car. He asked me in and made me an offer I couldn't refuse. Ralph put me up in a hotel, bought me food everyday, and trained me in blacktopping. I started out as a laborer in his business doing blacktopping work for him and ended up being a supervisor. I was paid very well. The better I became, the more he taught me. I learned to run his equipment and soon became so good at blacktopping that he sent me to work on the larger jobs he contracted in the larger cities of New York.

We rented a room in a motel 27 miles from the city in an area called Montgomery. I caught a cab into the city of Newburg on the weekends to party. The job was exciting, more for the new experience the weekends offered. In my stints to Newburg on the weekends, I met scores of women and smoked loads of crack. I was so high that I found myself staggering home through 27-28 miles of country terrain in New York back to the motel room we rented at two and three o'clock in the morning on several occasions. I would

Peter in his New York motel.

purchase a Greyhound bus ticket before the partying began so that I would have transportation back to Montgomery but I would be so stoned and having such a good time that I would go back to the Greyhound bus station to cash my ticket in for more money to buy more crack. I just couldn't let the party end until I spent my last penny. Somehow I staggered home safely each weekend and pulled myself together for the workweek that would follow.

I partied like this weekend after weekend, month after month, year after year. I managed to pull myself together well enough to perform during the week. I still can't figure out how I was able to keep up with the schedule Ralph planned for us in my condition. During the winter months, Ralph and I took his blacktopping business on the road. We traveled south, wherever it was warm, to find work. We went from New York to Texas, from Texas to Alabama,

Peter in New York on a blacktopping job.

from Alabama to Mississippi. After three and a half years of life in New York during the summer months and on the road in the winter months, I grew tired. It became harder and harder for me to keep up and Ralph began to notice. He pulled me to the side and pleaded, "Boss man, you need to get yourself together."

"Yeah," I replied helplessly, "I know it. It just seems like I can't stop, like I can't beat this habit." I truly felt helpless. I began to think more and more about home by this time and about how I could get my life back in order. I knew that if I could get home, things would be better but I had no money to get there. I smoked all of the money I earned. My helplessness quickly turned into hopelessness as I realized that there was nothing I could do in my own power to get myself out of the mess I made of my life. I knew the only hope for me was Jesus Christ so I prayed, "Lord, if You will save me, for real, if You will get me out of this mess, I will serve You."

CHAPTER 9
HOME SWEET HOME

Not long after, one of the Native American guys I befriended while living in the motel asked me to make a run to New York to buy drugs for him. His father died and he and his kinfolk needed something to help them cope with the loss. I was always the drug contact for my Native American friends. This was a very risky job because they usually asked me to purchase large quantities at a time. This occasion was no different. I was given a substantial sum of money and was off to Manhattan. On my way, I decided to take a detour, for good. I went to the Greyhound bus station I frequented so many times before and purchased a ticket to Ohio. I thought, "I'm going to get on this bus for home and never look back!" And I did, with nothing but the clothes on my back and the remainder of the money I was suposed to spend in Manhattan.

It was a long ride home. During the ride, I had plenty time to think about how things could be once I arrived in my hometown if I could just do right. I told myself, "Look, you've got a chance at a new life and you can't go home and mess up!" After scolding myself then convincing myself that I could do okay if

I tried really hard, I fell asleep. Before I knew it, the Greyhound bus pulled into my hometown bus station. I caught a cab to my mother's house and after taking a deep breath, knocked on the back door. I heard someone call, "Who is it?" I answered, "Chuckie." My mom and stepfather were afraid to let me in given my history of ruthless behavior. They were not sure of my mental condition because when I left going to Florida years earlier, I was in a terrible state. My mother knew I wasn't any better because I called her from New York several times crying, "Mom, help me! I don't know if I can make it!" Nevertheless, she welcomed me against my stepfather's wishes, stating firmly with a mother's love, "This is still my son." They took me in in good faith and I managed to stay clean for hours, then days, then weeks. Little by little they began to trust me again. I knew that I needed to support myself so that I wouldn't wear out my welcome so I began looking for work. For the first time, I had no desire to call up "Mari-J." God was moving.

I figured I was pretty good at blacktopping since I learned so much about the trade in New York working for Ralph. I went to a blacktopping company hoping they would need a laborer. The employer gave me an application and I completed it. He interviewed me and concluded the interview with, "Well, I'll call you later." I was anxious to work so this conclusion wasn't good enough for me. I needed to know right then if I could work or not so I interrupted and told him, "I need to know right now if you're going to hire me because I need to purchase a pair of work boots for the job." My persistence and eagerness impressed him so that he replied, "I'll tell you what. You go purchase those boots because you're hired right now!"

I went to work and worked very hard every-day, drug free. God was still moving. I also worked around the house *and* on my mother's heart, attempting to mend the breach I caused over the years. I started going to church with her in an attempt to mend the breach I caused in God's heart as well. One day while riding down the street with my mother, my then ex-wife, Shurnie, spotted me. She moved in with her mother after she divorced me. Her mother threatened to put her out of the house if she caught Shurnie seeing me ever again. Shurnie paid no attention to this threat. She stopped over my mother's house to find out if it was really me she saw in the car with my mother. She knocked on the door and I answered. I was totally surprised to see her. I didn't think she would ever speak to me again because of my total neglect and abandonment of her as a result of the control my reckless lifestyle had over me. I asked her in and we talked and talked and talked. We knew we couldn't see one another openly, her mom would have killed us both, so we arranged to meet in places we wouldn't be discovered in order to spend time together. We had lots of catching up to do so we met one another secretly every chance we got.

After awhile, we grew closer and closer and began dating all over again. I grew closer and closer to God as well. I continued to go to church with my mother while dating Shurnie. The more I moved toward Him the more He moved toward me until one night in church He filled me with the Holy Ghost. I was so full of His Spirit that I could not stop crying. I went home and cried all night until I fell asleep. I woke up the next morning at 5 a.m. to get ready for work and I began to weep even more and I couldn't stop! Finally, I had to call Shurnie to tell her what happened. I didn't want to call her so early at her mother's house but I had to tell her what happened to me. She answered the phone and after hearing me sobbing asked, "What's wrong?" I cried, "I got the Holy Ghost!" She was so happy for me and seemed to fall in love with me all over again. Over the next few months I attended church with her faithfully and she saw a great change in me. I saw a great change in me, the true change of heart I prayed for years earlier.

CHAPTER 10
A NEW CREATURE

Brother Aikins also recognized that I was a new creature. But he also sensed that I needed to be totally cleansed of demonic oppression by the spirits that bound me for years on end so that I could *keep* my change of heart. He took it upon himself to direct me in my cleansing process. He said, "Son, it's time for your cleansing to come forth. You are demon and devil oppressed and God put me in your life to help get you free." I was shocked. I thought I was totally free once I received the baptism of the Holy Ghost. I thought about it and realized that Brother Aikins was right. I was not *totally* free. There were still things that I held on to that were strongholds in my life. I needed to be purged so that I could go forth in God wholeheartedly. With Brother Aikins' one-on-one counseling and discipleship, I was purged, delivered and refilled with the Holy Ghost. Once I was totally purged and delivered, the wind of the Spirit rekindled the fire I once had for God and I exploded! I began to go into the community telling others about the God who restored me. I declared to all who would listen that God is truly a rewarder of those who diligently seek Him! I couldn't be stopped! My fire was unquenchable!

Not only was my fire for God rekindled, but also my fire for Shurnie. We remarried and began a

brand new chapter in our lives. We began to absolutely surrender our lives to God and He began to take us to a new level in Him. As the saying goes, "new levels bring new devils."

Peter and Shurnie in their second wedding ceremony.

This proved true in our lives for my wife learned from our family doctor that she wouldn't be able to conceive. We tried all kinds of medical interventions for months and nothing happened. I began to seek God. I prayed, "Lord, I sure would like to have a kid." The church mothers prayed with us and we all touched and agreed that Shurnie's womb would bear fruit. I focused even harder on God and sold out to Him in every area

Shurnie, at nine months pregnant, at her baby shower.

of my life in an effort to prepare myself spiritually to receive this miraculous conception and guess what?

You're right! Shurnie conceived and delivered a healthy baby girl we named Shonnon who is now nine years old, full of the Holy Ghost, attending private school, and winning her classmates to Christ!

Peter and Shonnon on Father's Day in 2001.

After this miracle, I began to do more for God than ever. The more I did for God, the more He revealed to me that He had a calling on my life but I was not exactly sure what the calling was. I joined a local Baptist church. The pastor saw the calling on my life and soon after I joined the church, the pastor invited me to serve as a deacon in the church! I was so grateful to be chosen to serve God in this way. I learned all I could about God and His church in this role and I served faithfully. I was only allowed to serve within the four walls of the church, however, and before long I became frustrated. I wanted the opportunity to share my testimony of God's delivering power in my life with sinners without the four walls but I could find no one to mentor me or even accompany me in taking my testimony to the streets for God. I didn't even know of any brothers or sisters in Christ who had been delivered from the streets as I had who could accompany me. Finally, after serving on the deacon board for four years, I resolved to hit the streets on my own, Bible in hand, fire still burning!

CHAPTER 11
HARD FALL, HARD LESSON

Off I went, alone, into the neighborhood crack houses, preaching the gospel and sharing my testimony with crack addicts. I felt I could at least get *them* delivered if no one else since I was once a crack addict myself. I preached and preached in the crack houses, sometimes the addicts put me out but I always went back. One day, while in a crack house, the smell of crack began to arouse the desire of my flesh. I felt I could beat the urge to take a hit of crack and ignored the warnings of the Spirit to leave. My defenses broke down the longer I lingered and I ended up smoking the very crack I claimed I had deliverance from just minutes earlier! I was so hurt. I mean so hurt that I "geeked," hard. I mean I totally freaked out. I literally lost my mind and began to scramble on the floor grasping for a crack pipe to get a high to assuage the devastation I felt of failing God when suddenly, there was a commotion in the crack house. The dope boys were ramping and raving over turf rights. They began shooting at one another and in the crossfire I ended up in a closet, naked, with two naked women.

Somehow, when I looked around and surveyed

the scene, I was shocked back into the real world by the shear degradation into which I had fallen in just a few short minutes. I prayed with my whole heart, "Lord, get me out of this mess!" I thought, "Here I am, a deacon in the church, in a closet with two naked women. What would the church say and think about this? What would the community say if the police arrested me and invited the news stations to report my arrest and the incident surrounding my arrest in the news? I'm supposed to be a witness for Christ!"

With this thought, I pulled my clothes back on and ran out of the crack house. I was utterly disgusted and disappointed in myself. I gave up all hope of ever receiving forgiveness for falling again, and being the man God called me to be. I decided to end it all. I stormed into my house, forced Shurnie out, grabbed my pistol, and shoved it to my head. I sat in the corner trying to muster up the strength to pull the trigger. In the meantime, Shurnie called for help. She, the neighbors, my mother, and other family members rushed over. She also called good old Brother Aikins. She knew that if anyone could help me, he could. While others stayed outside and prayed, Brother Aikins approached the house. He later told me that he was afraid to approach the house given my history but that

God told him to go inside. He said that God told him that the blood of Jesus covered him.

With this assurance, He walked through the garage to the door that led into the house. He tried to force the door open but couldn't. Brother Aikins said that he felt led to try to pull the door open. Just as he bent down a little in order to pull the door in with all his might, a knife came plunging through the wall and into the other side of the garage, missing Brother Aikins' face by inches! In sheer fear, I had flung a knife into the wall in an attempt to prevent anyone from stopping me from taking my life. Brother Aikins told me that at this point, he prayed again and asked God, "Lord, do You want me to proceed on?" God answered, "You are covered under the blood."

Somehow, Brother Aikins was able to get the door opened. A neighbor joined him and remarked, "I don't know if we should go in. This looks like a dangerous situation." Brother Aikins replied, "Dangerous or not, I'm going in." He came into the house, walked through the kitchen, and began to call my name. By this time, I disappeared into the basement. He called, "Where are you Chuck? I'm here. I'm here." He later told me that he knew that I was in the basement and that he prayed again and asked God, "Are You sure

You want me to go down there?" As he proceeded down the steps into the basement, trusting God for divine protection, God answered, "You are covered under the blood." He looked in all of the rooms in the basement. Brother Aikins reported after the incident that as he was checking each room of the basement, he was drawn to the furnace room where I was sitting, gun in hand, ready to pull the trigger. As he approached the furnace room, he remembered praying a third time, "God, do You want me to go in there? I know he has a gun." God gave the same answer, "You are covered under the blood."

Brother Aikins came into the furnace room and turned on the light. I warned, "Brother Aikins, don't come any further! I want to end it! I want to end it! I have failed! I want to end it!" Brother Aikins began to talk with me about the love of Christ and to pray in the Spirit. He also began to bind the spirit of suicide that gripped me and refused to let me go. Shurnie entered and joined him in prayer. As they prayed, Brother Aikins walked toward me and took the gun out of my hand. He put his arms around me and squeezed me as I balled in his arms. He continued to comfort me with the truth of God's love for me and to assure me that God still had a purpose for my life. He told me that God could still use me to bring life to many. I disagreed and mumbled, "No. I am a failure." Brother Aikins had heard enough and demanded, "Chuck, get up, go take a rest, and I will call you later on in the day. I am taking the pistol with me." I managed to get up and get some sleep. Brother Aikins left.

At about 4:30 p.m. later that day, Brother Aikins called as he promised and came over to talk with me. He put me on a program of counseling and purging from the spirits that bound me at that time. It was a hard road to recovery for me and for Brother Aikins as many more spirits had gained a stronghold in my life through my ignorance this time around than the last. Nevertheless, I broke free once again. Needless to say, this experience taught me a huge lesson. I learned not to go into the world without a brother or sister with me. Disobedience almost cost me my life. I vowed to always witness with another brother or sister in Christ as He commanded His disciples to do when He sent them out in Luke 10:1. What an awful way to learn a lesson. I can truly say that this is a lesson I will never forget.

CHAPTER 12
RESTORED TO PREACH THE GOOD NEWS

After being cleansed and restored, Brother Aikins encouraged me to continue serving on the deacon board. Through the years, I knew I had tapped into a piece of the will of God for my life but I knew there was more. God gave me the other piece through an evangelist who attended my church named Sister Betty. She, too, saw the fire in me and a calling in the area of prison ministry. She looked at me and said, "Chuck, the Lord wants you to go to the prison and give a testimony about the goodness of God and where He brought you from." Ready to serve God in any way that I could, I accepted the invitation from Sister Betty to go with her to a workhouse to share my testimony with the inmates.

My first experience sharing my testimony with inmates took place in this workhouse. Sister Betty and I arrived. She proceeded to minister to the inmates then called me forward to give my testimony. As I gave my testimony, God moved! The place ignited and the fire of the Holy Ghost fell! God began to deliver inmates everywhere! The altars were jammed packed from end to end as the power of God shook the very gates of hell! That day, God spoke to Sister Betty again and told her to take me into the prisons to give my testimony. I remembered the Scriptures in Psalm 119: 1 and 2 that read, "Blessed are the undefiled in the way, which walk in the law of the Lord. Blessed are they that keep his testimonies, and that seek him with their whole heart," and Romans 10:14 that reads, "How shall they call on him in whom they have not believed? and how shall they believe in him whom they have not heard? and how shall they hear without a preacher?" At that time, with those Scriptures in hand, I vowed to preach in the prisons the Gospel that God ordained for me to preach which is, and will always be, my testimony of His saving, delivering, and cleansing power in my life. I took every opportunity to go with Sister Betty into the prison to give my testimony.

I just couldn't keep still! My fire waxed hotter and hotter! All I wanted to do was share the Good News of Jesus Christ. I couldn't get enough of working for God so I branched out and went into the nursing homes to share my testimony with the residents there in addition to sharing in the prisons. I was so eager to help others to know this God I served, that I took an elderly woman from the nursing home to church every Sunday. This was a challenge because she was the meanest woman in the whole nursing home. It was also a challenge because she had no legs and sat in a wheelchair. Nevertheless, faithfully, Sunday after Sunday, I lifted Mrs. Clark into my truck, placed her wheelchair in the truck bed, and drove her to the church I attended. Eventually, Mrs. Clark saw Christ in me and allowed Him to heal her heart.

God arranged another divine encounter with a man I met named Brother William. His vision for the lost was similar to mine in that he was called to minister to drug abusers and prostitutes on the streets and to minister to the men and women in the Salvation Army facilities. He desired to develop a program that would bring these people into the church in order to disciple them as they made the transition from a sinful life on the streets to a new life in Christ within the church community. Brother William brought his vision before the deacon board of which I was a member. To my dismay, my fellow deacons were reluctant to adopt the program. They figured Brother William was just a young man with a lot of zeal and not enough experience to launch and maintain it. God allowed me to step forward in holy boldness as a representative of the deacon board to tell the deacons that God would bless the program if they gave the young man an opportunity. The deacons agreed to allow Brother William to develop the program and he is now touching lives through this program worldwide!

As I watched Brother William's ministry expand, God showed me the vision of small tents in the drug and prostitution infected areas being used as ministry bases from which to minister to those bound by this lifestyle. I shared this vision with the pastor of my church. He said, "Son, go prepare." He had indeed prepared me to preach and to rightly divide the word of truth but felt it was necessary to send me out to prepare for outreach ministry. I was excited that he gave me the green light to seek instruction to help me carry out my vision. I had no idea, however, just where I could find this instruction to help me prepare for this great work. I prayed that God would lead me in the right direction and on my way to a women's conference with Shurnie, He began to lead me in that direction just as I asked.

As we drove down I-75 to Cincinnati to the conference, we passed a church sitting off of the highway called Solid Rock Church. I was drawn to the church and I said to Shurnie, "You know what? One day we're going to stop at that church." Sure enough, on the way back from the conference, we pulled off of the highway and stopped in the church during a Sunday service. The pastor picked me out of the crowd and exclaimed, "Hey, you must be a preacher! Come up here and pray for this lady." As I made my way to the front, there stood a lady supported by a cane. I raised my hands to pray for her and before I could touch her, she collapsed under the power of the Holy Ghost. She got up off of the floor after basking in the presence of God awhile and walked away from the altar back to her seat without the support of her cane! I left the church after the service was dismissed moved in my spirit at how God used me in the life of a complete stranger. I determined in my heart to return to the church to see what classes were offered to help prepare me for the vision for outreach ministry in my own church and neighborhood.

In the meantime, I guy from my church intro-duced me to a group of men who held Bible studies in homes across the Dayton area. There I met the brother who led the Bible study. He happened to attend Solid Rock Church. As I continued with the men going house to house in the Bible study, the leader called me out and said, "Hey you, Peter. We've been wait-ing on you to come to this men's group. God said

He was going to send a brother by the name of Peter who would be the completion of this men's group." We talked after class and I told him of my vision and desire to train in the area of outreach ministry to carry out my vision in my church. He invited me to Solid Rock Church to check out the classes it offered. I found that there were several classes from which to choose. I took every class I could.. I took a class on basic Christianity, a class focused on fulfilling one's dream, and another on outreach ministry. I was so excited to learn how to make my vision a reality and how to minister effectively.

I immersed myself in these teachings and after nine months of specialized teaching at Solid Rock Church, I was eager to set my vision in motion and to teach others in my church what I had learned. I prepared myself as my pastor advised and was ready to launch out into the deep waters of inner city ministry! However, on my way to go to tell the pastor of my church what I learned, the Holy Ghost spoke to me and said, "Peter, I didn't bring you out of Egypt for you to go back!" When I heard this, I did as the disciple Peter did Jesus in the Bible. I rebuked the Lord, thinking that I heard Satan's voice, not God's, and that Satan was trying to keep me from going back to my church.

Of course, I ignored it and went on to my church as planned. I was determined not to let Satan steal what I learned over the past nine months nor let him steal my vision. I was off, full steam ahead!

When I arrived for the deacons' meeting, the deacons asked where I had been for the past nine months. I shared with them all I had learned and experienced at Solid Rock Church in preparation for ministry at the counsel of our pastor. Quickly the tables turned. I became a villain! It was clear that I didn't belong there any more and was not accepted after serving as a deacon for ten years! I said to myself, "Oh well, I'll just give my testimony to the congregation Sunday morning since the deacons won't receive me." Sunday morning came and I could hardly wait. It was time for the praise and worship to begin. (Mind you, I had been at Solid Rock Church for nine months so I had become accustomed to praising and worshipping wildly, dancing, spinning, jumping, the whole bit!) In stark contrast to the worship at Solid Rock Church, the Sunday morning praise and worship at my church was definitely not what I had become used to while worshipping at Solid Rock Church. Immediately, God spoke to me once again and said, "Peter, I didn't bring you out of Egypt for you to go back!"

I returned home with a sad face, never even getting the chance to share my testimony. My wife noticed my countenance and asked, "What's wrong, Honey?" I replied grimly, "Baby, I believe the Holy Ghost is changing me and moving me in a new direction." She replied, "Honey, God already spoke to me and told me that our time at our church is finished." Whew! I was relieved to know that God had spoken to my wife, too. This was a big decision as I was a deacon and she was the mass choir president! Nevertheless, at the leading of the Holy Ghost, I went to the pastor at the first opportunity and withdrew our membership. Without a comment, he gave us a written letter that officially served as our walking papers. With papers in hand, we walked, well ran, to Solid Rock Church.

CHAPTER 13
NEW HOME, NEW MINISTRY,
NEW LIFE

Excited to join Solid Rock Church, I took our letter to Lawrence Bishop, the senior pastor of Solid Rock Church. As I presented the letter from my former pastor, Pastor Lawrence declared in amazement, "I've never seen a dismissal done in such an orderly fashion! Son, we'll be taking membership in two weeks." Before he could say more, with all due respect, I reasoned with him. "Pastor," I said, "I just withdrew my membership from my old church. Now I'm not trying to change the rules and regulations but I'm uncovered, I'm naked! I ask that if you would be so kind, allow me to become a member of Solid Rock Church right now!" He said, "Son, you're a member right now!" He then announced from the pulpit, "Brother Peter is an official member of Solid Rock Church. He didn't want to wait for the membership class and I didn't want him to wait and that's okay. I knew God sent him but I just couldn't tell him!"

I was overjoyed and grateful to be received so warmly and with such open arms in our new church home. From that point, with a thankful heart, I began to attend services with my family regularly. After the ordeal I just endured, I wanted to just sit back and enjoy the services. And that I did! I danced and danced and danced during the praise services. I even found myself spinning after awhile! I could really spin! Oh, I could spin like a top by the unction of the Holy Ghost! I would spin for what seemed like five or six minutes at a time as fast as a human being could spin! God put a praise in me that I never experienced in my life and that I have never seen anyone else experience for that matter! And I'll tell you what; the more I would spin, the more I would feel the presence of the Holy Ghost. I was so happy to be able to spin and dance for the Lord. It's funny because I couldn't even dance when I was in the world. Now that I am on this side with Father God, I can dance . . . like David danced! I'm waiting for the day that I can dance 'til all my clothes fall off! I want to be all that God has called me to be as a praiser!

Six months passed, and to my surprise, Pastors Lawrence and Darlene gave me a designated seat on the front row, then later in the "Amen Corner" on the pulpit. This embarrassed me. It really embarrassed me. It also shocked me because (Can I be real?) a white man and a white woman never treated me with such respect in my entire life! I need to tell the whole truth so can I just tell it like it really was? I had a big problem with white folks and there was no way that I was going to be under the authority of a white woman, especially. Furthermore, as a deacon from a particular denomination, I had a huge problem with women preaching from the pulpit. One day, Pastor Lawrence was preaching and in his sermon he "read my mail." He said, "I want to tell you something. There are some people who have a problem with my wife as a woman preaching the gospel. But I want to let you know that Mary carried the Word for nine months!" Boy, did that blow my mind. Then he asked the congregation, "Who carried the first message to the disciples?" He answered himself, "Mary Magdalene, by the unction of the Holy Ghost." As he spoke, God spoke to my spirit and said, "I *did* call women to preach." I mumbled to myself, "Oh, Lord. I guess that fixes me up real good." So, by the Word and the Spirit, I was able to accept the truth. God took me through yet another cleansing, this time from the spirits of racism and sexism, so that I would be totally delivered from these generational bondages. Thanks be to God!

Not soon after, Pastor Darlene came to me and said, "I had a dream that you were over the prison ministry here at Solid Rock Church." I said sheepishly,

"Oh Lord. Here we go." I knew God was about to uncover me after being buried for so long in my former church. I knew prison ministry was my calling but God hadn't spoken to me clearly so I didn't move. Two weeks later, Pastor Lawrence came to me and said he had a vision that I was over the prison ministry at Solid Rock Church, too. I thought, "Oh, Lord. They've teamed up on me now," and prayed earnestly, "God, if You spoke to them, surely You can speak to me. And I'm not moving God until *You* speak to me." I left

Peter and Pastors Lawrence and Darlene Bishop.

church and went home that Wednesday night after service and prayed again, earnestly, "Lord, You spoke to them. I ain't moving 'til You speak to me." That night, I said, *that night*, I fell into a trance. While in the trance, God showed me a glimpse of myself over the prison ministry at Solid Rock Church! After that, I moved wholeheartedly to begin to fulfill His purpose for my life. And as I moved, He provided all I needed to get the job done, namely, His anointing. I began to see thousands upon thousands saved, set free, and delivered just as I was. In 1999 and 2000, the prison ministry team led nearly 3,000 souls to Christ each year. In 2001, the prison ministry team shared the Gospel in seven juvenile facilities, five county jails, twelve prisons within the state of Ohio, and three federal prisons and led over 7,000 inmates to Christ!

In 2001, we also traveled out of the country to the mountains of Haiti in an area steeped in witchcraft to minister to the natives. The head witch doctor in Haiti heard that we were in town. He and his followers planned to come against the "missionaries" they heard were visiting. While our ministry team was ministering in the local church, he and his followers came in toting machetes and handcuffs planning to

The Solid Rock Church Prison Ministry Team in 2001.

escort us out of Haiti. I just happened to be praying and preaching when they arrived. Before they laid a hand on us, the Holy Ghost spoke to the witch doctor and suddenly he and his followers put their machetes and handcuffs back in their holsters and took a seat.

When the invitation was given for sinners to come to the altar and give their lives to Christ, the witch doctor came forward and confessed that Jesus Christ is Lord and prayed the Sinner's Prayer! After the service ended, we all moved outdoors. The witch doctor noticed that there was mud on the feet of one of the women who traveled with us. He got on his knees in the mud and washed her feet with his bare hands!

In 2002, the 30-member ministry team hopes to share in over 90 federal prisons! In many of the prisons, we will conduct three- and four-day revivals! We will even host the first singing group formed of former inmates of London Correctional Institution to sing in a local church service. This has never been done in a prison in the state of Ohio. Needless to say, ministry demands will soon outgrow the ability of our 30-member team to handle! Isn't God good? Give Him a hand praise now as you read this book for His mighty acts through me, a once fatherless child and hopeless inmate!

God has not only blessed me spiritually with the anointing to carry out His work in the prison mission field, He has also blessed me materially. I can't remember the last time I was broke! I have my own business, own a home, and send my daughter to a private school. I now write checks legally that I can cash instead of forging them. God even spoke to me and told me that I would be a millionaire after bills are paid by the end of 2001. I am the same man who could not read or write but who now supervises thirty staff members as head of a thriving prison ministry under the leadership of Pastors Lawrence and Darlene Bishop by the guidance of the Holy Ghost! If God can do all of this for me and through me, how much more can He do for you?

I can't praise God enough for the wonders He has performed in my life through His Son, Jesus Christ and the power of the Holy Ghost. The Pharisees asked, "Can any good thing come out of Nazareth?" Yes! And His name is Jesus Christ, Who was, is, and is to come! I was told that nothing good would ever come out of me. Many people said to me, "Boy, you ain't nothing. Your daddy was nothing and so are you!" It is true that my earthly father came up short in more ways than one but my heavenly Father more than compensated where my earthly father lacked and because God is my Father, I *am* something. I am the apple of His eye, His son, and I will live up to all that He created me to be. Now I ask you, "Can anything good come out of you?" Yes! The Jesus in you! The same Jesus that brought good out of my life can bring good out of your life no matter how difficult your situation. God specializes in working out for His good the situations in life that seem impossible.

I can't give you all of my testimony either in one book because God is still overtaking me with blessings, even as I speak. His blessings in my life cannot be contained in one book! I will have to bring you up to speed in my next book. I just wanted to take time to begin to tell you about a man who was fatherless and who owned seven penitentiary numbers until he met the Father for whom he had been searching for years!

CHAPTER 14
JAILHOUSE RELIGION:
CAUGHT AND KEPT

It is not very hard to believe that inmates are receiving Christ by the thousands, as many figure that "jailhouse religion" is easy to "catch." Given the desperate situations in which many prisoners find themselves, Christ seems the only hope, especially while in jail. "If Christ can provide solace," many ask, "what would it hurt to accept Him while in prison? The test of true salvation is loyalty to Him once released."

This is a fair question. I was even faced with this cynicism when I was released from prison and shared with my family my new faith in Christ. Like me, thousands have been released from federal prisons, state prisons, and juvenile facilities and are presently faithful church members, committed husbands, fathers, mothers, and diligent employees who are serving God with all of their heart. Former inmates are truly enjoying the spiritual *and material* blessings God provides in addition to their freedom. However, the best way to address this concern is to share a testimony of "religion" that was "caught" and kept by an inmate touched by the power of God through the prison ministry team of Solid Rock Church.

Brother Ed Hobson is the man. He now serves on my prison ministry staff and shares his testimony with thousands. His testimony was featured in the Solid Rock Church newsletter and I included it in this book so that you can read about how God performed the miraculous in Ed's life.

Brother Ed's Testimony

I met Brother Peter on July 22, 1997. I was on lockdown in a jail cell for 90 days on federal conspiracy charges with the intent to possess and to distribute heroine. The tiny cell cramped my style and by this time I desperately needed to stretch my legs. I figured, "The only way I'll get a break from this hole is to ask to see a chaplain." I submitted a formal request to see a chaplain and soon after a correctional officer walked to my cell and called, "Ed! You have a clergy visit!" "What's a clergy?" I called back. "A clergy is a chaplain," the correctional officer replied. "You must've requested him or he wouldn't be here!"

The correctional officer escorted me to the room where Brother Peter was awaiting my arrival. When I saw him I thought, "Who is this guy here?" He didn't look at all like what I imagined a minister would look like. He looked just like an average guy. He looked just like me! Apprehensively, I introduced myself and he did the same then opened our meeting with prayer as I listened.

After he prayed, he began to share his testimony with me. The more he talked the more it seemed that he experienced the same things I was going through at that time. The anointing of the Holy Ghost was evident as I lingered in Brother Peter's presence. The words of life he spoke so touched my heart that I began to cry like a baby. Brother Peter sensed that my heart was receptive to the gospel of Jesus Christ as he shared. He also sensed that I was ready to receive Christ in my life if only he would lead me. And he was right. At his leading, I prayed the Sinner's Prayer, and became, at that moment, a new creature in Christ. Old things passed away and all things became new!

We were both elated about my conversion. Brother Peter congratulated and encouraged me and vowed to visit me the next week. When he returned, he gave me a Bible and a Bible study course from Solid Rock Church called, "Building on the Rock." Through this course, I learned the foundational truths of the Bible and how to walk out this new Christian life and Brother Peter discipled me every step of the way. Through his weekly shepherding, my daily Bible reading and faithful chapel attendance, I grew stronger and stronger in my faith in Jesus Christ. I was truly a changed man.

Before long, the weeks became months, the months became one year, and one year became two years and I was still incarcerated anticipating my sentencing. During this time I also prayed a lot, particularly for my wife, Shira, who was in the free world struggling to care for herself and our three children I left behind. I asked God to provide for them since I couldn't and to shield them from a life of suffering as a result of my sins. God answered this prayer in a huge way. I called home one day and Shira explained how she and the kids were blessed with a home on three and a half acres of land! They were enjoying the home and the kids were having a ball playing outside in the bright, warm sun on the plush, green grass. Boy how I wished I were there with them but it wasn't God's time yet. Soon it would be.

Time progressed. I continued in Bible reading, church attendance, and prayer, still awaiting my sentencing. My prayers seemed always to focus on my wife and children. My heart lingered there, as I was so concerned about their well-being. I decided to cast my cares on God concerning my family and God proved again that He is Jehovah Provider. I called home on another occasion only to learn that my wife was blessed with a new car! Needless to say, I rejoiced with a thankful heart, praying that I would be reunited with my family real soon. Little did I know that God's timing was quickly approaching the horizon.

It was May of 1999, the month I was scheduled to appear in court to receive my sentence. I faced thirteen years in a federal prison for the charges against me. After a short deliberation, the judge sentenced me to the full thirteen years I deserved. I was distressed. Before ordering that I be escorted out of the courtroom to begin serving my thirteen-year prison sentence, the judge asked if I had anything to say. I bowed my head and gave thanks to God then I began to speak. I shared my testimony of deliverance from a life of irresponsibility and lawlessness to a new life of accountability and righteousness in Christ. I spoke for what seemed to be thirty or forty minutes. The spirit of God spoke through me and moved on the judge's heart as I declared the goodness of God in the courtroom.

When I finished, miraculously, the judge reduced my sentence by nine years! Praise God! This meant I had only one year left to serve! I served three years awaiting my sentence and the three years I served was counted toward the thirteen years I had on the books! God is awesome. He spoke through me in the courtroom and proved Himself once again. This time He proved Himself as Jehovah Defense Lawyer!

I rejoiced all the way back to the prison and into my cell. The goodness of God was almost too much for me to contain. Yet the countdown was on . . . 365 days to go before I would be a free man! It was decided that I should serve the rest of my term in a federal correctional institution in West Virginia so I was packed up and escorted to West Virginia. My days were numbered! I rejoiced as I counted down.

Pretty soon, four months passed. For some reason, really nothing short of the grace of God, I was summoned back to Ohio by the judge who sent me to West Virginia. When I appeared before him in the courtroom, he said, "Mr. Hobson, you've had enough. You're free to go." I could hardly believe my ears. I was free, free to be with my family! God had answered my prayer to be reunited with my family in a way that was exceedingly and abundantly above all that I could ask or think!

The day I walked out of that prison in late December 1999, I called Brother Peter and Brother

Kevin, a guy on the prison ministry team who visited me occasionally while I was incarcerated. I wanted to be sure to have Christian brothers to support me in my transition from life behind bars to life in the free world. They invited me to the New Year's Eve celebration at Solid Rock Church, the church they both attended. I was eager to attend and planned to do so with my wife and three children. I rushed home and embraced my family. It was a great reunion but somehow incomplete without my church family.

After greeting one another, I told my wife of my desire for us to bring in the new year as a family with our church family worshipping God and thanking Him for my safe and miraculous return to our family. She agreed to go and we had a blast! The worship and the word of God delivered that night seemed to take our family to a higher height and deeper depth in Christ. We were ready to build our family anew, this time on the Rock (that is, Christ Jesus) at the Rock (that is, Solid Rock Church).

All was well. I immediately settled into the role of husband and father. I was thankful that God provided for the needs of my family through others in my absence and now it was time for me to take on the role as provider for my family as God intended. I renewed my driver's license so that I would have transportation to and from work and called Brother Peter for direction concerning job prospects. He told me about an organization called Workplace Reconnection. He explained that this organization helped ex-offenders find gainful employment. I contacted this organization and immediately secured a job paying $5.60 per hour. I knew this hourly wage would not be enough to care for a family of five but I was thankful anyway for the opportunity to work and made up my mind that I would work hard for God in this position until He promoted me and increased my wages.

I worked very hard and was a faithful employee. I was also a good steward of the $5.60 per hour I earned as I paid my tithes, gave offerings, and cared for myself and for my family. As I worked, I quoted Matthew 25:23 which reads in the King James Version, "His lord said unto him, Well done, thou good and faithful servant: thou hast been faithful over a few things, I will make thee ruler over many things: enter thou into the joy of thy lord."

One day my faithfulness was tested. I was having an extremely hard day at work. My boss began to increase my workload significantly with no mention of a pay increase. He expected more and more of me and

I met his expectations with flying colors, neverthe-less, he never breathed a word about promoting me. I was ready to quit! I called Brother Peter to vent my frustration but he was not home. His wife, Shurnie, answered the phone. She asked what the matter was and I told her. She ministered to me and encouraged me. She quoted Matthew 23:25, the same Scripture I had been quoting since I took the job and said, "You can't quit now. You're just going through a test because one day you're gonna be the boss in there."

She was right. I stood the test and remained faithful and just five months later, I was promoted to plant supervisor on the management team and was given a considerable salary increase! God is so faith-ful to His word! Not only was I blessed with a pay increase, I was later given favor with a bank loan offi-cer who wrote me a check to purchase a new car!

For years I lived life as a career criminal. Statistics report little hope for career criminals to reform and live life as productive members of soci-ety. But God said, "Not so 'cause I've got another plan for Ed. I'm going to save him, return him to his family, save his family, bless him with a new job and a car, and send him back to the prisons to deliver his brothers and sisters by the power of God through his testimony." And God did just that. You see, when God moves in your life, no devil in hell can stop Him. I thank God for men of God like Brother Peter who answered the call of God on July 22, 1997 to return to the prison to visit and disciple me. Since then, I have never been the same.

CHAPTER 15
YOU CAN, TOO

Of course, this is just one testimony of a former inmate who was saved behind bars and who continues to live for God on the other side of the prison walls. Yes, there are many inmates, like me, who left the faith once the pressures of the real world set in. God promised that trials would come to test the faith of those that are His but that He would always provide a way of escape (I Corinthians 10:13).

I encourage you, brothers and sisters, to look for the way of escape God provides when you are tempted. Don't make the same mistakes I did. At a point after my release, I began to "play church" and in my playing I lost the very Spirit that would help me find this way of escape. I allowed myself to become entangled over and over again in the bondage I left behind. I took on spirits that are in the world designed to destroy me. These spirits are real and can also be found in the church where they are ready to attach themselves to those who are not sincere and faithful in their relationship with God.

If you are in a backslidden state, know that it is not too late for God to deliver you. If God did it for me, He can do it for you. I pray that God will send someone wherever you are to help you in your journey with Him. I pray that you will turn from your wicked ways and turn to the ways of God. The Bible says in Romans 10:9 in the King James Version "That if thou shalt confess with thy mouth the Lord Jesus, and shalt believe in thine heart that God hath raised him from the dead, thou shalt be saved." God's word cannot return to Him void so the good news is you can recommit your life to Christ and be the light He created you to be for Him in this dark world if you confess Him as Lord of your life. You can make a difference in someone's life for God if you let God cleanse you. He wants to use you as a witness for Him just as He uses me, Brother Ed, and countless other former inmates to help set other captives free. Will you let Him use your life for His glory?

I am so thankful that God impressed upon the pastors of Solid Rock Church to bless me with the honor of being used for His glory on the prison ministry team. As God placed my pastors in my life to be a blessing to me, God wants to place someone in your life to be a blessing to you. Through this book, I pray I will be one He chooses to be a blessing to you. Be encouraged by His work in my life, and allow God to change *your* life in the name of Jesus Christ. Amen.